Q Quarto Knows

Inspiring | Educating | Creating | Entertaining

Brimming with creative inspiration, how-to projects, and useful
information to enrich your everyday life, Quarto Knows is a favorite
destination for those pursuing their interests and passions. Visit our
site and dig deeper with our books into your area of interest:
Quarto Creates, Quarto Cooks, Quarto Homes, Quarto Lives,
Quarto Drives, Quarto Explores, Quarto Gifts, or Quarto Kids.

The Animal Awards © 2019 Quarto Publishing plc,

Text © 2019 Martin Jenkins.

Illustrations © 2019 Tor Freeman

First Published in 2019 by Frances Lincoln Children's Books,

an imprint of The Quarto Group.

400 First Avenue North, Suite 400, Minneapolis, MN 55401, USA.

T (612) 344-8100 F (612) 344-8692 www.QuartoKnows.com

A catalog record for this book is available from the British Library.

ISBN 978-1-78603-779-4

The illustrations were created using pencil and digital color

Set in Futura

Published by Rachel Williams and Jenny Broom

Designed by Karissa Santos

Edited by Lucy Brownridge

Production by Catherine Anastasi

Manufactured in Shenzhen, China PP052019

9 8 7 6 5 4 3 2 1

FSC
www.fsc.org

MIX
Paper from
responsible sources
FSC® C001701

THE
ANIMAL
AWARDS

Written by Martin Jenkins
Illustrated by Tor Freeman

Frances Lincoln
Children's Books

WELCOME TO
THE ANIMAL AWARDS!

The ceremony is about to begin. Roll up, roll up, roll up! The ceremony is about to begin so prepare to be amazed. We're here to celebrate the *crème de la crème* of the animal kingdom, and shine a spotlight on the finest achievements and unique qualities of some special individuals. Among others, we will be awarding prizes to the fastest, the oldest, the strongest, the smelliest, the tallest, and the longest. We have some unusual prize winners and some quite scary ones, too. As we run through our short lists you'll have the privilege of meeting our esteemed guests from dangerous, frogs to organised ants, to spiders that have devised all sorts of strange and admirable ways of catching their food.

It's been a really difficult job choosing winners but we hope you approve and find plenty to marvel at in this beastly line-up of champions.

Now put your hands together and clap! *The Animal Awards is about to begin...*

The Nominees for the Animal Awards Are:

8
Mound-building termite

10
Great bustard

12
Chimpanzee

14
Peregrine falcon

16
Deep-sea anglerfish

18
Emperor penguin
Giant Pacific octopus
Wandering albatross
African elephant

20
Earthworm

22
Leafcutter ant

24
Cuvier's beaked whale

26
Lion

28
Chameleon

30
Arctic tern
European eel
Blue whale
Caribou

32
Bat

34
Skunk

36
Tiger

38
Electric eel

40
Giant panda

42
Honeybee
Naked mole rat
Gray wolf
Clownfish and sea anemones

44
Beaver

46
Spider

48
Kangaroo

50
Giraffe

52
Poison dart frog

54
Superb lyrebird
Pistol shrimp
Woodpecker
Puerto Rican coquí

56
Cheetah

58
Dung beetle

60
Vulture

62
Tortoise

64
Ostrich

66
Caribbean reef squid
Peacock flounder
Scarlet kingsnake
Orchid mantis

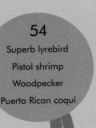
68
Lion's mane jellyfish

70
Axolotl

72
Giant clam

74
Polar bear

76
INDEX

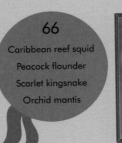

MOUND-BUILDING TERMITE

Category: insects | **Native to:** tropical areas around the world | **Lives for:** over 30 years in the case of some queens, non-queens much less | **Diet:** dead plant matter and fungi

Termites don't look very impressive—most of them are less than half an inch long—but boy, can they build!

Termites build some of the most impressive natural structures, called termite mounds. They can reach heights of over 30 feet.

Termites, like ants and honeybees, are social insects. They live in big colonies with a queen, a king, and hordes of soldiers, whose job is to defend the colony from attackers. There are workers that do everything else, such as locating food and water, digging tunnels and building, and doing repairs.

The mounds come in a variety of shapes and sizes. However, the termites live in nests in the ground below them. It's not clear why they build mounds, but some scientists think it is a clever way to circulate air. During the day, the outside of the mound warms up and expands, which pushes fresh air down into the nest below. Through the night, the outside of the mound cools and contracts, which forces stale air out through tiny holes in the sides.

The AMAZING ARCHITECTURE AWARD

A termite constructs towering mounds using natural materials, such as soil and chewed-up wood, mixed with their saliva.

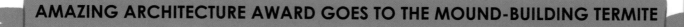

AMAZING ARCHITECTURE AWARD GOES TO THE MOUND-BUILDING TERMITE

Their mounds are built to last. Some mounds in Brazil have been standing for over 3,500 years.

They are crafty. At least one species of termite produces a chemical that we use in mothballs. Termites use this to kill mound invaders.

They think big. A large nest can house several million termites.

They are clever. Scientists still don't completely understand how termites organize themselves when they build such complicated structures.

9

GREAT BUSTARD

Category: birds | Native to: Europe and Africa | Lives for: ten years | Diet: omnivore

The FABULOUS DISPLAY AWARD

Many of the most spectacular show-offs are birds, but none beat the great bustard. It shows off for one main reason: to try to attract a mate.

As with most flashy animals, the males are the worst culprits. They are basically saying to any prospective mates nearby, "Look at me! I'm the best! I'm the healthiest and the fittest. Choose me!"

They're big—standing up to 3 feet tall and weighing up to 44 pounds—making them one of the heaviest flying birds alive today. In spring, at the start of the breeding season, a male's feathers become more brightly colored and he grows a pair of large, white feathery neck whiskers. When displaying, he inflates a balloon-like structure called a gular pouch in his throat, cocks his tail forward over his back, and twists and spreads out his wing feathers. He either stands still while doing this or struts slowly about, stomping his feet.

The effect of all this it to make him look rather like a giant animated powder puff—it's dramatic and absurd at the same time, but it gives the females a chance to decide which male they like best. They'll then mate with him in the hope that their young will inherit his strength and fitness.

Great bustards have long feathers near their beak that make them look as though they have a little mustache-like beard. This helps them look pompous and stately.

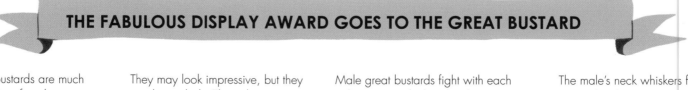

THE FABULOUS DISPLAY AWARD GOES TO THE GREAT BUSTARD

Male great bustards are much bigger than females.

They may look impressive, but they are lousy dads. They play no part in looking after the eggs or young.

Male great bustards fight with each other to see which is the dominant one in that group.

The male's neck whiskers first appear when he is two years old. Every year they grow, reaching full length when he is six or seven.

10

Great bustard males gather together to display at sites called leks. Leks are out in the open so females can see them from a long way away, and males can spot predators before they get too close.

Other kinds of bustard also have remarkable displays. The lesser florican, which breeds in India and Nepal, lives in long grass. To be seen, the male leaps into the air, flapping furiously and then dropping down again.

Australian bustard males have huge feathery neck pouches, called gular pouches, which touch the ground.

A male houbara bustard puffs up its white throat feathers, tucks its head back, and sprints forward as if it's in a hurry.

CHIMPANZEE

Category: mammals | **Found in:** Western and Central Africa | **Lives for:** 35 years in the wild, 50 years in captivity | **Eats:** almost anything, mostly fruit

For a long time, it was thought that only humans used different tools. However, it turns out that chimpanzees are also multi-tool-using champions.

Some animals use one tool for one specific purpose. Egyptian vultures, for example, pick up stones in their bills and throw them at ostrich eggs to break open the tough shells. Woodpecker finches use cactus spines to spike tasty grubs, and sea otters balance flat stones on their stomachs, which they use to smash open mussels and sea urchins. A few animals use several different tools for different purposes. Among these the champions are clever old chimpanzees.

The types of tools used vary between chimp groups across Africa, but there some things they all do. They make sponges out of scrunched-up bundles of leaves for soaking up drinking water, and they throw missiles, usually stones but sometimes poop, mostly at rival chimpanzees. They also use tree trunks as drums to communicate with each other. Chimpanzees don't just use tools, they make them, too. To extract tasty termites from their nests, they make fishing rods. They do this by picking a thin branch from a tree, peeling off the bark, splitting it along its length, clipping it with their teeth at one end to make a sharp point, and fraying it at the other to make a brush. It's laborious, but clearly worth it for a termite treat!

Chimpanzees use combinations of tools, which hardly any other animals do.

THE NIFTY TOOL-USER AWARD GOES TO THE CHIMPANZEE

Chimpanzees are human's closest-living relatives—it's not surprising that we share a lot in common, including tool use.

Chimps are cunning. A chimp who lived in a zoo used to hide rocks in piles of straw in his enclosure when he thought no one was looking. They would be on hand to grab and throw at visitors the next day.

Some chimpanzees make whole tool kits—in Gabon, Central Africa, they use five different implements in a specific order to get honey out of wild bees' nests.

In some places, chimpanzees use flat stones as anvils, a type of heavy iron block, and smaller stones as hammers to bash open hard, tasty palm nuts. If the anvil becomes wobbly or uneven, they'll wedge a smaller stone underneath to steady it.

New Caledonian crows are smart tool-using birds. They turn splinters of wood, pine needles, or pieces of fern stem into different-shaped hooks for snagging grubs out of tiny crevices.

Orangutans are the only other animals to use several tools in the wild. They use thin branches to poke around in tree holes for things to eat. They use leaves as gloves when handling spiny fruits and as napkins for wiping sticky plant juices off their chins.

PEREGRINE FALCON

Category: birds | **Found in:** almost everywhere, except Antarctica and New Zealand |
Lives for: 15 years in the wild | **Eats:** mainly other birds

There's a clear winner for the title of world's fastest animal, and that is the peregrine falcon.

This handsome bird of prey feeds almost entirely on other birds, which it hunts in the air. It cruises around quite slowly on the lookout for likely prey, or sometimes keeps watch from a high perch. When it spots a flock of birds, it rises high into the sky above them, and when the moment is right, it folds its wings back and goes into a headlong dive called a stoop. It picks one bird from the flock and, aiming an outstretched, clenched talon at one of the bird's wings, swoops toward it. A direct hit will usually stun or kill the victim. The peregrine then slows down and turns to catch the bird in midair, before flying off to pluck and eat it at leisure.

Peregrine falcons can fly at amazing speeds while diving—easily over 200 mph—and probably quite a lot faster. Scientists have calculated that they could reach nearly twice this speed at high altitudes, where the air is thin, although no one has actually measured. The stoop has the advantage of giving the falcon the element of surprise, and the high speed of the dive makes it more maneuverable. If the intended prey spots the falcon approaching, it will likely not be able to escape!

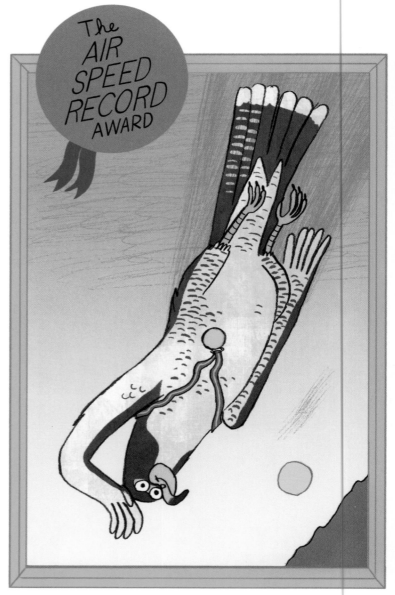

Peregrine falcons reach incredible speeds thanks to gravity.

THE AIR-SPEED RECORD AWARD GOES TO THE PEREGRINE FALCON

They have a transparent third eyelid that keeps their eyes free of grit and dust when they're diving.

The peregrine falcon's speed has made it a very successful bird—it's the most widespread bird of prey.

Female peregrine falcon's are much bigger than males, but they are both equally speedy.

Young peregrines spend quite a lot of time practicing their stoops—it must be pretty unnerving for any nearby starlings or pigeons.

DEEP-SEA ANGLERFISH

Category: bony fish | Found in: deep seas all over the world | Lives for: not known, but probably about 25 years | Eats: other smaller sea creatures

The deeper you go below the surface of the sea, the darker it gets, even in the middle of the day.

That's because sunlight is absorbed by seawater. Very little of it reaches farther down than 650 feet. Most living things in the deep sea can produce their own light. This ability to make light is called bioluminescence. Some land animals can do it, too, for example fireflies, glowworms, and some fungi.

It is believed that some animals produce light so that they can see where they are going, and others use it to attract mates. It can also be a form of defense, with the light acting as an alarm. An animal will use a flash of light to scare off any attackers. This may also attract larger predators that will attack the other animal.

Female deep-sea anglerfishes are believed to take advantage of this. Most female anglerfish have a luminescent organ on a long spine growing from the back or head, called an esca. She dangles this in front of, or above her head, like a lure. Other approaching animals that think there might be a tasty snack usually find themselves snapped up in her razor-sharp toothy jaws.

The Enlightenment Award

There are over 200 types of anglerfish, and most of the females have a glowing growth on their heads.

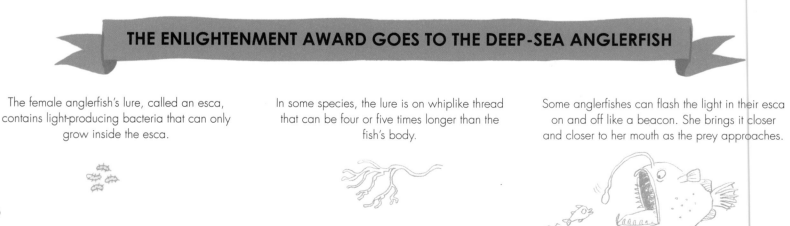

THE ENLIGHTENMENT AWARD GOES TO THE DEEP-SEA ANGLERFISH

The female anglerfish's lure, called an esca, contains light-producing bacteria that can only grow inside the esca.

In some species, the lure is on whiplike thread that can be four or five times longer than the fish's body.

Some anglerfishes can flash the light in their esca on and off like a beacon. She brings it closer and closer to her mouth as the prey approaches.

17

All animals have offspring—without young, their species would die out! There are lots of different ways that animals reproduce. Often a male and female will only meet when they mate and then the female lays her eggs or gives birth. Some animals do things differently and go to great lengths to give their young the best possible start in life. Here are some of the most impressive.

EMPEROR PENGUIN *Aptenodytes forsteri*
The cool dad award

Category: birds | **Found in:** Antarctica | **Lives for:** usually 20 years, sometimes up to 50 | **Eats:** fish, squid and krill

When penguins look after their young, it is often the mother that gives most of the care, but not always. Emperor penguins breed on the Antarctic ice in the autumn. When a female has laid her egg, she turns around and heads out to sea to feed. The father keeps the egg warm through the freezing winter. He doesn't eat at all during this time, but he has enough fat on him to survive. When the mom returns in early spring, the chick will hatch and the dad goes off to sea to find food himself. The mom looks after the chick until he returns.

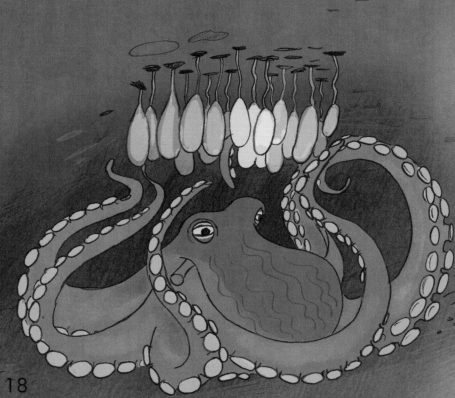

GIANT PACIFIC OCTOPUS
Enteroctopus dofleini
The mom-of-the-year award

Category: mollusks | **Found in:** North Pacific Ocean | **Lives for:** 3–5 years | **Eats:** other sea animals

The female giant Pacific octopus makes the ultimate sacrifice when looking after her young. She lays eggs only once in her lifetime, but she produces 400,000 eggs in one go. She glues them to a sheltered underwater spot and tends them continuously, guarding them from predators. She wafts seawater over them to make sure the baby octopuses growing inside get enough oxygen, and she cleans off any seaweed that might start to grow. She doesn't eat for the six months it takes for the eggs to develop, and when her brood has safely hatched, she dies.

18

WANDERING ALBATROSS *Diomedea exulans*

The loyal couple award

Category: birds | **Found in:** Southern Ocean | **Lives for:** over 50 years | **Eats:** fish, squid, and krill

Like many seabirds, wandering albatrosses form long-term partnerships, with the same pairs coming together each breeding season to raise their chicks. This takes a long time. The egg has to be incubated for 11 weeks before it hatches, and the chick then needs to be fed constantly for about nine months. However, things don't always go according to plan: the egg may fail to hatch or the chick might die, in which case the birds will return the next year to try again. If this happens to other species of seabirds, the pair will split up. Albatrosses stick together.

AFRICAN ELEPHANT *Loxodonta africana*

The great-grandmother award

Category: mammals | **Found in:** Africa | **Lives for:** at least 70 years | **Eats:** herbivore

African elephants generally live in families, sometimes quite big ones. These families are made up of females and young. Grown-up males mostly live with other males or by themselves. The oldest female in the family is in charge, and she is called the matriarch. She makes decisions about where the group will go next, defends the group if danger threatens, and will discipline the youngsters. The other elephants are usually her younger sisters, daughters, nieces, granddaughters, and great-nieces. Her sons, grandsons, nephews, and great-grandsons will be around, too, until they are teenagers, when they leave.

19

EARTHWORM

Category: segmented worms | **Found in:** almost everywhere, except Antarctica | **Lives for:** eight to ten years | **Eats:** fallen leaves and other plant remains, manure, compost

Soil is incredibly important. It's what almost all plants grow in, and without plants we simply wouldn't be able to survive.

Soil is made from a mixture of minerals from broken-down rocks and organic matter from living things. It is home to a huge range of living things, including roots from plants, microbes, fungi, and many creepy-crawlies and grubs. Some animals feed on plant roots, killing or stunting the plants we see on the surface. Other animals play a major part in keeping the soil in good condition for plants to grow. The champions at this are earthworms.

Earthworms live in underground burrows and feed on organic matter, either in the soil or on the surface. Some of them venture to the soil surface at night to collect fallen leaves or animal manure, which they drag down into their burrows to eat in the comfort of their own home. When they eat, they also take in mineral grains that help crush up their food. Their digestive systems extract goodness from the food and they poop out the waste as a fine mixture of undigested organic stuff and mineral grains. Worm poop is called "cast" and is rich in the chemicals that plants need. It is in a form that is easy for plant roots to absorb.

A worm's poop is full of soil-enriching goodness.

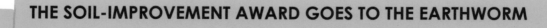

THE SOIL-IMPROVEMENT AWARD GOES TO THE EARTHWORM

The burrows that earthworms make keep the soil open and airy, and help water to drain away quickly after heavy rain.

Most earthworms are less than 10 inches long, but giant Gippsland earthworms from Australia can grow to over 10 feet in length.

One normal-sized earthworm can produce over 9 pounds of cast in a year. In rich soils, there can be over 400 earthworms in a square yard.

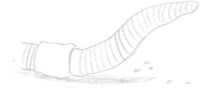

Earthworms lay eggs in a cocoon under the surface of the soil. The hatchling earthworms are tiny but very strong—they can push 500 times their body weight in soil out of the way when they are burrowing.

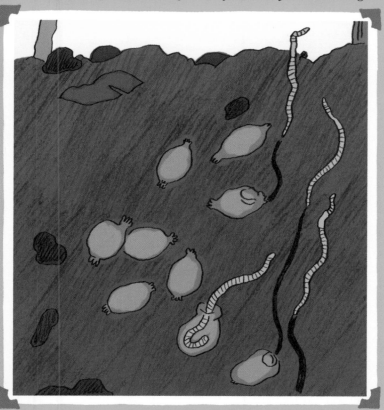

Earthworms come in different colors. The giant blue earthworm from northern Australia is, you guessed it, bright blue!

Most earthworms live near the soil surface, but some make burrows up to 6 feet deep. Others live in piles of dead leaves high up in tropical trees.

Earthworms are food for all sorts of other animals, including birds, frogs, salamanders, hedgehogs, shrews, and moles.

LEAFCUTTER ANT

Category: insects | **Found in:** South, Central, and North America | **Lives for:** probably up to 20 years (queens only) | **Eats:** fungus and plant juices

It is easy to think that humans invented farming, but ants have been at it for tens of millions of years.

The descendants of these agricultural pioneers are still around today. The most sophisticated of which are leafcutter ants, found in forests in warm parts of South, Central, and North America.

Leafcutter ants live in underground colonies. Each colony has one queen and lots of worker ants. The queen spends her entire life laying eggs, which hatch into more and more workers. To feed the colony, the workers have to farm their food. They do this by carrying leaf pieces back to their nest and chewing them into a pulp. Fungus eventually grows on the rotting pulp and produces clusters of tiny, nutritious globules, which the ants eat. The globules are also eaten by the grub-like baby ants, called larvae, that eventually grow into adult ants themselves.

Most of the larvae become female worker ants without wings, but during the breeding season—usually when the long rains start—some of them grow wings and become young queens and winged males. The young queens and winged males fly away from the nest to go and start their own new colonies.

The INNOVATION IN AGRICULTURE AWARD

A leafcutter ant turns leaves into tasty nectar to feed its friends by harnessing fungus power.

INNOVATION IN AGRICULTURE AWARD GOES TO THE LEAFCUTTER ANT

A big colony can contain eight million workers, so they need farm a lot of food to keep them all full!

When she leaves her original colony, a young queen ant takes some fungus with her in her mouth to start a fungus garden in her new colony.

Worker ants chew the leaves into balls for the fungus to grow on. They poop on the balls, which contains chemicals that break down the plant material, making the fungus easier to use.

Leafcutter ants keep their fungus gardens incredibly clean and well weeded. There are ants whose only job is to deal with waste disposal.

Worker leafcutter ants are divided into castes, or groups, based mostly on size. Each caste has a different job. The biggest are soldiers, who defend the colony. The smallest are gardener-nurses, who tend the fungus gardens and look after the larvae, which live in the gardens. Medium-sized workers forage for leaves and flowers.

Foragers collect leaves from trees and shrubs near the nest. They cut leaves and flowers into pieces and carry them as far as 200 feet back to the nest. Smaller workers hitch a ride. Their job is to shoo the flies that attack the foragers and to clean the plant pieces.

CUVIER'S BEAKED WHALE

Category: toothed whale | **Native to:** all over the world! | **Lives for:** 50 years | **Diet:** carnivore

The world's champion diver is a Cuvier's beaked whale. Its longest and deepest dive recorded so far lasted for an amazing 2 hours and 17 minutes, with a descent of nearly 10,000 feet below the surface of the sea.

All animals need oxygen to stay alive. A Cuvier's beaked whale is an air-breathing animal and gets its oxygen from the Earth's atmosphere.

When it goes underwater, it has to take enough oxygen with it. Most animals that breathe air but spend most of their lives in water need to come to the surface every few minutes to breathe, which limits how far down they can dive. Cuvier's beaked whales are different because they have become specially adapted to survive long, deep dives.

The whales dive to these depths in pursuit of prey, and their favorite food is squid. It is too dark here for them to hunt by sight. Instead, they use a technique called echolocation. The whale sends out a call by making a rapid clicking noise. This bounces off objects nearby, and it listens for the returning echoes, which allow it to locate and identify these objects.

This clever diver is relatively new to the hall of fame, with scientists only discovering how deep it could dive in 2014.

THE DEEP-SEA DIVER AWARD GOES TO CUVIER'S BEAKED WHALE

Cuvier's beaked whales can store a lot of oxygen, not only in their blood but also in other parts of their bodies.

They breathe out before diving to reduce the amount of gas in their lungs. This makes them less buoyant so they can dive quickly.

When they are diving, they shut down their digestive systems and organs such as their kidneys so that they use less oxygen.

When they divert their blood supply away from their extremities to their brain and heart so that these can keep working.

Elephant seal –
100 mins ; 2,400 m

Emperor penguin –
32 mins; 535 m

Sperm whale – 90 mins; 2,250 m

Leatherback turtle – 70 mins; 1,300 m

After a really deep dive, a Cuvier's beaked whale stays near the surface for at least 40 minutes before diving again. This is because it has built up harmful chemicals in its body during the dive, which need to be processed by breathing in plenty of oxygen.

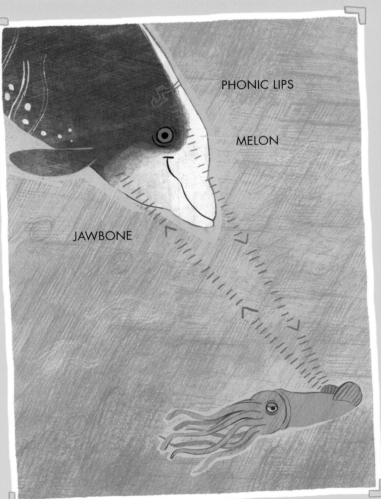

PHONIC LIPS

MELON

JAWBONE

A beaked whale makes clicking sounds by blowing air through openings called phonic lips to track prey. The sound passes through an oil-filled organ, called a melon, in the whale's forehead. It picks up the returning sounds through its lower jaw.

LION

Category: mammals | **Native to:** Africa and India | **Lives for:** around 12 years |
Diet: carnivore

The male lion's mane is the most famous and most impressive. Lions are members of the big-cat family, and they are the only type of cat that has a mane.

Quite a few different animals have manes, including horses, giraffes, and maned wolves. The lion's mane is special because it is a sort of advertisement—it shows how strong and fit the animal is. The longer and darker the mane, the more impressive the lion. Both male and female lions pay attention to the condition of a mane. It helps females to choose a mate and males to decide which lions to fight with.

Male lions are likely to do quite a lot of fighting during their lives. Small numbers of them roam around trying to take over existing groups, called prides, by driving away the resident males. Unsurprisingly, the resident males resist this, and fierce, sometimes fatal, fights can break out. However, male lions usually avoid picking fights with other males that have longer and darker manes than their own: these lions are likely to be stronger and fitter, so they risk coming off badly in any fight.

The MARVELLOUS MANE AWARD

A lion's mane will keep growing throughout its life.

THE MARVELOUS HAIR AWARD GOES TO THE LION

Female lions are more attracted to darker manes, but they don't seem that fussy about the length.

Male lions decide whether they will fight another lion based on the length and color of its mane.

A long, dark mane can cause its wearer to overheat, so male lions that live in very hot places have short, pale manes.

It's possible that male lions first evolved manes to help protect their necks and shoulders when they were fighting each other.

Male lions that live in prides usually leave the females to do all the hunting. They make sure they get all the best bits of the kill, though!

Prides usually consist of a few males, several females, and their cubs. On average, there are 15 lions in a pride, but there can be up to 30. In some places, prides are much smaller, with just one male and a few females.

Life in a pride can be tough. When males successfully take over a pride, not only do they drive away other adult males.

Female lions usually stay in the pride they were born in. Male lions are driven out when they are two or three years old. They become nomads for a few years before trying to take over an existing pride.

27

CHAMELEON

Category: reptiles | Found in: Madagascar, Africa, southern Europe, and parts of Asia | Lives for: up to ten years, perhaps more | Eats: insects and other small animals

Tongues are used for tasting and drinking and, if you're a human, for speaking with. Mostly though, they help animals to eat.

Animals like salamanders, anteaters, and some frogs and toads use their tongues to catch their prey. But the champion, who has turned its tongue into the best hunting device, is the chameleon.

Chameleons are lizards. There are about 200 different kinds, most of which live in Madagascar, a big island off the east coast of Africa. They use their remarkable eyesight to hunt insects. Their eyes bulge out from the sides of their head and can move separately from each other. This gives them all-around vision, and means they can follow two different objects at once. When a chameleon has spotted its prey, it slowly stalks it. When the prey is in range, the chameleon takes careful aim and opens its mouth, sticking its tongue a little way out. Then: thwack! Out shoots the tongue, and in a flash, the victim is dragged into the chameleon's mouth, where it is usually briefly chewed before being swallowed.

The RIDICULOUSLY LONG (AND STICKY) TONGUE AWARD

Some chameleons have tongues two and a half times the length of their body.

THE RIDICULOUSLY LONG (AND STICKY) TONGUE AWARD GOES TO THE CHAMELEON

A chameleon's tongue can reach speeds of up to 16 feet per second.

A chameleon's tongue has a wide flattened end covered with saliva, which is about 400 times as sticky as human spit.

Big chameleons can use their tongue to catch birds, other lizards, and even small mammals.

Chameleons are harmless to people, but in Madagascar many people fear them, thinking that they have magic properties.

The largest chameleon is called Oustalet's chameleon, and it is about the size of a small cat.

The smallest chameleon is the Brookesia micra. It is just 1 inch long, half of which is its tail.

Many chameleons can change color. Sometimes they do this for camouflage to hide from predators, but usually they do it as a signal to other chameleons, often to show that they are ready to fight or to mate.

29

Many animals like to live in small areas or territories, but others travel across the world in spring or autumn, which is called migration. They migrate to find warmer weather, to breed, or because they are looking for food. Often these animals spend a part of their life in one place and then move somewhere else. Many migrating animals make journeys each year, while others only do it once in their lifetime.

ARCTIC TERN *Sterna paradisaea*
The far-flung flier award

Category: birds | **Found in:** parts of the northern hemisphere during the breeding season | **Lives for:** 35+ years | **Eats:** small fish

The Arctic tern is a seabird that nests mostly in the Arctic circle, but also farther south in North America and Eurasia during the northern hemisphere's summer months. It migrates all the way to the Antarctic in time for the southern hemisphere's summer. These birds don't follow a direct route and some have been tracked covering 60,000 miles in a single round-trip—that's more than twice around the world!

EUROPEAN EEL *Anguilla anguilla*
The get-a-wriggle-on award

Category: fish | **Found in:** Europe, the Mediterranean and North Africa as adults | **Lives for:** 80 years | **Eats:** other animals

European eels are long fish that live in the fresh waters and along the coasts of Europe and North Africa. When they are ready to breed, adult eels swim in a wriggling motion an extraordinary 4,000 miles across the North Atlantic to the Sargasso Sea near the USA. When the tiny see-through young hatch, they swim the long way back toward Europe, changing in appearance as they do so. When they reach the coast, they look more eel-like, but are semi-transparent and are called glass eels.

30

BLUE WHALE *Balaenoptera musculus*
The long-distance caller award

Category: mammals | **Found in:** Pacific, Antarctic and Atlantic oceans | **Lives for:** 80+ years | **Eats:** carnivore

Blue whales are the world's largest animal. They swim over vast distances, but it's not known whether they make regular migrations or not. They can, however, communicate over long distances. They do this by making very loud, deep sounds; so deep that humans can't hear them. In the past, blue whales were able to hear these sounds from 1,000 miles away. The distance over which the whales can hear each other is thought to have shrunk dramatically, because their sound is drowned out by noise from human sources, such as shipping and the sonar radar from submarines. What exactly the whales are communicating to each other is a mystery; it's possible that it is mainly males advertising their presence to prospective mates.

CARIBOU *Rangifer tarandus*
The walking-for-weeks award

Category: mammals | **Found in:** North America and Eurasia | **Lives for:** up to 17 years | **Eats:** lichens, grasses, and other low-growing plants

Most long-range migrants fly or swim because there are fewer obstacles in the air and in the sea than on land. An exception is the caribou, or reindeer, of Alaska and Yukon in Canada. They spend the winter in valleys in mountain ranges, but as the winter snow starts to melt in spring, over 200,000 caribou begin a 1,500 miles trek north to the coast where the females give birth. The journey takes ten weeks, with pregnant females arriving first and males and the previous year's young arriving later.

BAT

Category: mammals | **Found in:** all continents, except Antarctica | **Lives for:** 40 years | **Eats:** usually flying insects, also fruit, flowers, fish, and blood

Most flying animals, including insects and birds, need some light to steer by; they use the stars, the moon, or streetlights. Bats don't have this problem, and are perfectly at home in the pitch black.

This is because they aren't using their eyes to see where they are going. Instead, they have perfected the technique of using sound to navigate by—we call this technique sonar, or echolocation.

Echolocating bats have extra-sharp hearing and an make high-pitched noises in their voice box or larynx. When it is flying in the dark, the bat produces a series of these high-pitched noises through its mouth or nose. The sound waves bounce back off nearby objects and the bat picks up the returning echo sound; this helps it to build up a picture of where it is and which objects are nearby. In this way, it can avoid bumping into things when flying at night and, in most cases, track down its food. The majority of echolocating bats feed on insects that only come out at night and bats are expert at using sonar to find them.

A bat will use sonar to fly around at night without crashing, as well as for spotting tasty snacks.

THE NIGHT-FLIER AWARD GOES TO THE BAT

The largest-known bat colony is made up of 20 million Mexican free-tailed bats in one cave. They use sonar to avoid bumping into each other.

Mexican free-tailed bats hold another record: they have been clocked flying along at 99 mph, faster than any other recorded animal.

The world's smallest bat is Kitti's hog-nosed bat from Thailand. It weighs just 2 g and is 1 inch long. It rivals the Etruscan pygmy shrew for the title of world's smallest mammal.

The saying "Blind as a bat" isn't accurate at all. Bats can see very well, and fruit bats have much better vision than humans.

Vampire bats are famous for coming out at night to hunt for blood. They mostly feed on cows and horses. As well as using echolocation, they have heat sensors located around their noses, which guide them to warm blood.

Most of the 1,200 kinds of bat are small and eat insects. The largest bats feed on fruit. Most fruit bats lack the sophisticated sonar of their smaller relatives.

Bats love to eat moths, but moths have good hearing and try to escape. Some moths are cunning and make sounds that block the bat's sonar. The barbastelle bat has found a way around this: it whispers when echolocating so that moths don't hear until it's too late.

Some other animals use echolocation, too. For example the oilbird, some kinds of swiftlet, shrews, tenrecs, and quite a few whales.

SKUNK

Category: mammals | **Found in:** the Americas and southeast Asia | **Lives for:** up to ten years | **Eats:** mostly worms, insects, and other small animals

There are a dozen different kinds of skunk, and all of them are smelly.

Actually, that's not quite true—most of the time skunks don't smell particularly bad. But all of them are capable of producing a bad smell when they need to. At the base of a skunk's tail are two glands that store a pale yellow liquid. When threatened by another animal, such as a hungry bear or a wolf, the skunk will turn its back, raise its tail, and squirt out two jets of the liquid straight at its opponent. Skunks are good at aiming and can shoot the stinky jet 10 feet or more. The liquid smells awful, and also causes intense pain and even temporary blindness if it gets in an animal's eye. A direct hit will often put the attacker out of action long enough for the skunk to makes its escape. What's more, the smell lingers for days on fur, so the unfortunate predator is likely to have problems hunting afterward, as other animals will be able to detect its presence.

Not surprisingly, it doesn't take many encounters with a skunk for most animals to learn to steer clear. The skunk's striking black-and-white markings act as a signal to animals to keep away. These markings show up particularly well at night, when skunks are usually active.

A skunk squirts a foul-smelling liquid at any animal that doesn't respect its personal space.

THE REALLY SMELLY AWARD GOES TO THE SKUNK

Skunks have a special reserve of stink spray that lasts for four or five attacks, after which it takes up to ten days to replenish the supply.

Some people used to think that bathing in tomato juice would get rid of a skunk's smell. In reality, you need strong chemical cleaning products!

Baby skunks can spray when they're just eight days old. They can't aim properly until their eyes open after 24 days.

The great horned owl can swoop down from above and seize a skunk before it has a chance to fire back.

As well as having recognizable markings, skunks usually warn off predators by hissing and stamping their feet. The spotted skunk has an extra-special technique. It stands onto its front legs and dances around with its bushy tail spread out like a fountain.

Most skunks live in the Americas, but two kinds live in Asia: the Sunda stink badger, which is the smelliest type of skunk, and the Palawan stink badger, which has a distinctive stripe.

When disturbed, rather than using its stink gland, a Palawan stink badger often plays dead.

TIGER

Category: mammals | Found in: Asia | Lives for: up to 15 years in the wild, usually less | Eats: carnivore

Tigers are the biggest living members of the cat family.

Like all cats, tigers are hunting animals, and when they are not hunting, they love to spend time asleep. They are also among the most endangered of all large animals. It's not hard to figure out why: nowadays there are an awful lot of people in areas where tigers are found—or used to be found—and tigers and people don't mix very well. Tigers need lots of space, and a good supply of food, such as deer, antelopes, and wild pigs, which are becoming rarer due to overhunting by people. The tigers habitats have been cleared for farming and building on as well. Where wild animals are in short supply, tigers are likely to hunt goats, cattle, and other domestic animals, and sometimes even humans. This tends to make the tigers targets for local people. There are other reasons that tigers are hunted: their skins are sought after as trophies and their bones and other body parts are a valuable ingredient in traditional Chinese medicine.

Tigers are protected by law in all the countries where they live in the wild, and selling tiger products is banned under the Convention on International Trade in Endangered Species (CITES). Even so, illegal poaching and smuggling still continues, and now tigers are very rare.

The ENDANGERED HUNTER AWARD

Tigers are excellent hunters, but sadly they have been hunted by humans, so there are very few left.

THE ENDANGERED HUNTER AWARD GOES TO THE TIGER

Tigers used to be found all over Asia, from Turkey in the west to the Russian Far East. Now they only live in a fraction of this area.

Around half the world's wild tigers live in India. There are probably between 1,700 and 2,300 there.

Tigers hunt medium-sized prey but occasionally attack animals much larger than themselves, such as rhinos, and elephants.

Tigers usually ambush their prey, lying in wait and suddenly pouncing.

There are plenty of candidates—too many—for this award. Other endangered hunters include:

Borneo
Bay Cat

Darwin's Fox

Red Wolf

African
Wild Dog

Iberian Lynx

In places with plenty of food like Northern India, a tiger's range might be 3 square miles, but in the frozen Russian Far East, it may roam over 60 square miles. They are mostly solitary creatures, although sometimes a tiger will allow other adults to share its kill.

Tigers mostly live in forested areas that provide cover for them to hunt in. Unlike most cats they love to swim, and cool off in ponds and rivers in the heat of the day.

ELECTRIC EEL

Category: fish | **Found in:** South America | **Lives for:** 10–15 years | **Eats:** other animals

We tend to think of electricity as coming from plug sockets, batteries, or lightning bolts, not from fish.

However, electricity is vital to living things. Animals' nervous systems and muscles are powered by electrical impulses. These impulses create electric fields around an animal. Some animals can detect the fields made by other animals and use this information either to find prey or avoid predators. Others have special organs that make electric fields specifically for communicating with each other and for sensing everything around them. A few have taken this even further and use electricity as a weapon! The most extreme example is the South American electric eel, which isn't actually an eel, but a relative of the catfish.

This big freshwater fish makes two different kinds of electric field. One is a weak, low-voltage charge for sensing things and communication, and the other is strong (up to 600 volts), which it uses to catch its dinner. When an electric eel detects something tasty with its low-voltage field, it approaches its prey and releases a volley of very short powerful impulses that paralyze it so that it can be swallowed easily. If the prey is big, the electric eel often curves around it in a C shape, which intensifies the power of the shock.

The South American electric eel is a charged-up, 6-foot-long zap maker!

THE SHOCKING AWARD GOES TO THE ELECTRIC EEL

Unusual for a fish, an electric eel breathes air. They drown if they are kept completely underwater.

An electric eel can deliver a powerful shock, but it lasts for so short a period that it's extremely unlikely to kill a person.

The majority of an electric eel's body is given over to electricity-generating organs.

A male electric eel makes a foam nest out of saliva, where the female lays 3,000 eggs. He looks after the eggs until they hatch.

If an electric eel is threatened by an animal, it launches an attack. It holds its chin against the animal's body, while firing off shocks. If the animal is out of the water, it creates a much more painful sensation than an underwater attack.

Most electro-sensing animals live or hunt underwater. However, the long-beaked echidna from New Guinea has around 2,000 electro-sensing organs in its snout, which it uses to find earthworms in damp soil and fallen leaves.

These fish all make strong electric shocks that can stun prey or scare away predators. However, none are as powerful as the electric eel.

GIANT PANDA

Category: mammals | Native to: China | Lives for: 20 years in the wild | Diet: bamboo

Wild giant pandas eat just one thing—bamboo. And they eat lots of it, over 25 pounds a day.

They are members of the bear family and their closest-living relatives are all meat-eaters, like the polar bear, or are omnivores, which eat a whole range of animal and plant matter. So it seems an odd diet for a panda. A giant panda's digestive system is similar to that of other bears and doesn't appear to be well suited to a totally vegetarian diet. What's more, bamboo is a poor food source, with little protein and a lot of indigestible fiber—which explains why they need to eat such a lot of it to get the nourishment they need.

Specializing in such an unusual food source does have its advantages, however. Bamboo grows extremely widely in forests in China and other parts of Asia, and so pandas usually have a plentiful supply of food. It is tough and poor in nutrients, and few other animals eat it, so the giant panda doesn't have many competitors.

Several different kinds of bamboo grow in the region in China where giant pandas live, so they do have a very slightly varied diet.

A giant panda's diet is mostly made up of bamboo.

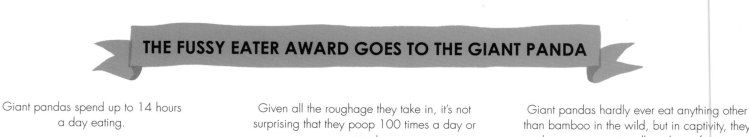

THE FUSSY EATER AWARD GOES TO THE GIANT PANDA

Giant pandas spend up to 14 hours a day eating.

Given all the roughage they take in, it's not surprising that they poop 100 times a day or more!

Giant pandas hardly ever eat anything other than bamboo in the wild, but in captivity, they are happy to occasionally tuck into fruit, eggs, honey, rice, or fish.

Giant pandas are rare, mainly because so many of the forests where they used to live have been cleared for farming. However, thanks to conservation efforts, there are probably around 2,000 in the wild, compared with fewer than 1,500 30 years ago.

Pandas are well adapted to process large quantities of bamboo. They have strong teeth and powerful cheek muscles for chewing. They also have an extra thumb on their front paws. This helps the panda to grip the bamboo firmly.

A baby giant panda is tiny, weighing just 0.2 pounds or so when it is born. It first starts eating bamboo when it is about six months old.

Other fussy eaters: monarch butterfly caterpillars only eat milkweed. Egg-eating snakes just eat eggs. Numbats only eat termites. Greater gliders will only eat buds on eucalyptus trees.

Some animals live alone, and are often hostile to other animals, including members of their own species. Others are much more sociable, living in groups where they collectively look for food and defend each other from predators. Occasionally, two completely different kinds of animals will work as a team.

HONEYBEE *Apis spp.*
The hard-worker award

Category: insects | **Found in:** almost everywhere, except Antarctica | **Lives for:** queens for up to eight years, workers for less than a year | **Eats:** pollen and nectar from flowers

Honeybees live in big colonies with just one breeding female, the queen. There are some males called drones and up to 30,000 worker bees in a single nest. The worker bees guard the nest and build cells out of wax for the queen's eggs to hatch in. They also collect pollen and nectar from flowers to eat and make honey out of. The honey is used for food in winter and to feed the bee larvae as they grow. One hive can make over 90 pounds of honey in one summer, which takes over a billion visits to flowers and about 2 million miles of flying in total.

NAKED MOLE RAT *Heterocephalus glaber*
The underground community award

Category: mammals | **Found in:** East Africa | **Lives for:** up to 30 years | **Eats:** mostly underground plant tubers

Naked mole rats are amazing for all sorts of reasons, apart from appearing incredibly ugly to us. They are extremely resistant to diseases, and they live for a very long time. They live underground in colonies of around 75. Only one female, called a queen, and a few males in the colony breed. The others all help look after the queen's young. They also feed them with their own poop!

42

GRAY WOLF *Canis lupus*
The pack-hunter award

Category: mammals | **Found in**: North America, Europe, and northern Asia | **Lives for:** up to 20 years | **Eats:** mostly medium-sized or large animals, such as deer and bison

Wolves live in family packs, consisting of a breeding pair of wolves and their children. The group lives and hunts together. By working as a pack, wolves can chase down large, powerful animals such as bison, moose, and musk oxen that would be dangerous to tackle alone. Wolves often howl, which is a signal for them all to gather together to go hunting.

CLOWNFISH *(genus Amphiprion)* **and** SEA ANEMONES *(Stichodactylidae family)*
The unlikely duo award

Category: fish and cnidarian | **Found in:** Indian and Pacific Oceans | **Lives for:** 30 years or more (clownfish); at least 80 years, probably much longer (sea anemone) | **Eats:** mostly small animals (clownfish); small animals, clownfish poop, and food from algae growing inside it (sea anemone)

Sea anemones have stinging cells called cnidocytes that they use to catch prey and defend themselves with. This method of defense doesn't always work, and some animals, such as bristleworms and butterfly fish, feed on sea anemones. Brightly colored clownfish are immune to the stings from cnidocytes, and take up residence among the sea anemone's tentacles. They chase off the sea anemone's predators and are in turn protected from their own predators by the sea anemone.

43

BEAVER

Category: mammals | Found in: North America and Eurasia | Lives for: usually five to ten years in the wild | Eats: plant matter

Beavers are very good at gnawing things, and the reason for this is because they have amazing teeth.

Most mammals, including humans, have two different sets of teeth. The first set, known as milk teeth, falls out as the animal is growing and is replaced by the second set. Once these new teeth are fully formed, they usually stop growing, which means that if they get worn down from chewing on hard material, or if they get broken or fall out, they can't be repaired or replaced.

However, beavers only have one set of teeth that never stops growing. This means they can chew away on hard objects without worrying because new tooth material will replace any that gets worn away. Their front teeth, called incisors, are especially well adapted for gnawing things. They are long and chisel-shaped, with flat, sharp ends, and they are self-sharpening.

Beavers are true landscape engineers, and they use their teeth to change the world around them to suit their needs. They do this mainly by felling trees, and they couldn't do that without their truly terrific teeth.

The TERRIFIC TEETH AWARD

A beaver's teeth look orange because they contain iron, which makes them super strong.

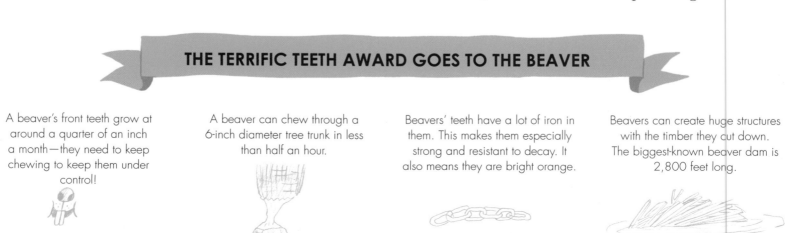

THE TERRIFIC TEETH AWARD GOES TO THE BEAVER

A beaver's front teeth grow at around a quarter of an inch a month—they need to keep chewing to keep them under control!

A beaver can chew through a 6-inch diameter tree trunk in less than half an hour.

Beavers' teeth have a lot of iron in them. This makes them especially strong and resistant to decay. It also means they are bright orange.

Beavers can create huge structures with the timber they cut down. The biggest-known beaver dam is 2,800 feet long.

44

Beavers have been known to cut down trees with trunks over three feet wide. It can take a family of beavers several seasons to fell a tree this big.

In the autumn, a beaver family stores tree branches in the pond near the entrance to their lodge. They spend the winter tucked up in their lodges, making occasional trips to their underwater larder.

Beavers build dams across streams to make ponds. They then build wooden lodges with underwater entrances in the ponds. As well as tree trunks and branches, they add mud, stones, bark, and leaves, which they carry with their front paws, to their dams and lodges to make them as waterproof as possible.

SPIDER

Category: arthropods | Found in: everywhere, except Antarctica | Lives for: sometimes over 20 years (goliath bird-eating tarantula) | Eats: mainly insects, also other small animals

Quite a lot of animals produce silk, but the champion silk-makers are spiders. There are over 45,000 different kinds of spider, and as far as we know, all of them produce silk.

Spiders make silk in special organs called spinnerets, which have tiny openings called spigots. The silk starts off as a liquid that moves through the spinneret and solidifies as it is pulled out of the end of the spigot. The spider pulls the thread out by using its legs or by attaching the end to an object and moving away. Most spiders can make several kinds of silk, some sticky and some not. Different spiders use their silk for different purposes. Some use it to line their burrows, and others wrap their eggs in it to protect them. Many use lines of silk as bungee cords or as parachutes for traveling through the air. Some, of course, use them to make webs for catch flying insects for dinner. Mostly, they use two different kinds of silk, one strong and non-sticky for the outer rim and main spokes, and the other type is very sticky and stretchy to make the mesh for trapping prey.

A spider spins a fine silk that is stronger than steel.

THE SPINNING AWARD GOES TO THE SPIDER

Tarantula spiders can produce sticky silk from the soles of their feet that helps them keep a grip when they are climbing slippery surfaces.

The oldest-known spider's web is a tiny piece trapped in amber and is 99 million years old. We know from fossils that spiders were spinning webs 300 million years before that!

Webs quite quickly lose their stickiness and become less effective at catching things. Spiders usually replace all or part of them pretty often, sometimes every day. Often they eat the old web so as not to let it go to waste.

Darwin's bark spider from Madagascar produces the strongest substance in nature. It uses it to make huge webs—some are nearly 30 square feet and reach across rivers and ponds.

The water spider lives in a waterproof diving bell made out of silk attached by threads to underwater plants. It fills the bell with air from the surface.

Spider silk is stronger than steel and a lot tougher because it can stretch. It is so light and fine that a thread long enough to go around the world would only weigh 1 pound.

Bolas spiders attract moths by releasing chemicals called pheromones into the air. When a moth approaches, the spider swings a sticky globule at it and the moth becomes dinner.

KANGAROO

Category: mammals | **Found in:** Australia and New Guinea | **Lives for:** up to 25 years | **Eats:** plants

A lot of animals can jump: fleas, grasshoppers, frogs, springbok, snow leopards. But the most famous jumping animals are kangaroos.

Not only can they leap a long way in one hop, they can reach really impressive speeds and cover many miles without stopping—most other animals, even those like frogs and fleas that use jumping as their main means of moving, only manage a few jumps at a time.

One of the main reasons kangaroos are so good at jumping is because they bounce. They have a very long, strong tendon in each leg called an Achilles tendon. This is made of a tough rubbery material that stores energy when it is squashed, in the same way that a rubber ball does. When a kangaroo lands from a leap, the tendon is squashed, then returns to its original length, releasing the stored energy as it does so. This helps push the kangaroo into its next leap.

It's not just their springy tendons that make kangaroos so good at jumping—they have very powerful back leg muscles and a long tail to help them balance.

A kangaroo is the bounciest creature on the planet.

THE BEST BOUNCER AWARD GOES TO THE KANGAROO

A big kangaroo can cover 30 feet in a single leap.

Kangaroos can reach hopping speeds of up to 40 mph, though they prefer to travel at 16 mph or so.

Kangaroos are very efficient hoppers, using small amounts of energy to travel a long way.

Kangaroos are very acrobatic when they jump: they can turn through 180 degrees in a single bound.

When a kangaroo walks, it doesn't use four limbs, but five! Its muscular tail is the fifth limb, pushing the kangaroo forward in the middle of each pace.

Some kangaroos live in trees. They are generally slow and clumsy on the ground but are expert climbers, leaping from branch to branch, using their long tails to balance.

Kangaroos belong to a group of mammals called marsupials. When they are born, baby kangaroos are less than an inch long. A newborn kangaroo uses its front legs to haul itself up its mother's stomach, where there is a pouch that it will stay in for months, until it is big enough to hop on its own.

GIRAFFE

Category: mammals | **Found in:** Africa | **Lives for:** 25 years in the wild | **Eats:** leaves and shoots

Being as tall as a house may sound inconvenient but it certainly has its uses, and the giraffe carries it off with elegance.

It has long legs, a relatively compact body, and an incredibly long neck. Its long dark eyelashes, swishing black-tipped tail, and gorgeously patterned coat help it stand out as an elegant fashionista.

Giraffes are elegant in most of their movements, too, in particular their walk, which has an easy, swinging gait. Unusually for a four-footed animal, a walking giraffe moves both legs on one side of its body and then both legs on the other side—most animals move the legs on the opposite side, that is back left at the same time as front right, to give them better balance. A giraffe's long legs and short body mean that its legs would risk getting tangled if it tried to walk like that. When they run, giraffes bring their back legs forward outside the front legs, again to minimize the chance of entanglement.

Even giraffe fights look surprisingly graceful. Males compete with each other using their necks. Each takes it in turns to curve his neck back and swing his head at his opponent, landing heavy blows until one or the other calls it a day.

Although a giraffe has a long neck and legs, the main trunk of its body is relatively small.

The TERRIBLY TALL AND ELEGANT AWARD

THE TERRIBLY TALL AND ELEGANT AWARD GOES TO THE GIRAFFE

With a maximum height of about 20 feet, giraffes tower over their nearest rivals, African elephants.

The giraffe's long legs and neck allow it to reach tasty leafy shoots high up on thorn trees, which are out of reach of other animals.

Male giraffes are taller than females and have stronger, more heavily built heads and necks—useful for fighting with.

Every giraffe has a different pattern to its coat—each one is unique, like a human fingerprint.

The only time giraffes don't look elegant is when they drink. They have to stand with their front feet far apart or half kneel to reach the water.

Even a newborn giraffe is taller than an average adult human. It can stand as soon as it is born, and can run within a few hours.

The giraffe's only closest-living relative is the okapi, which lives in rain forests in the Democratic Republic of the Congo. Okapis aren't tall, but they are elegant!

51

POISON DART FROG

Category: amphibians | **Found in:** South and Central America | **Lives for:** 20 years in captivity, less in the wild | **Eats:** ants, termites, spiders, mites, and all other small animals

Animals use poison for two main reasons: to attack and eat other animals, and to defend themselves.

Some combine the two. Rattlesnakes, for example, use the poison in their fangs to kill or paralyze their prey, but also to strike back at animals that might want to make a meal of them. They warn approaching intruders of their presence by rattling their tails. This may be enough to frighten away a potential predator before it attacks, helping the rattlesnake avoid a potentially dangerous or even fatal encounter.

Poison dart frogs only use poison to defend themselves, but they are extremely deadly. Some contain enough poison to kill ten adult humans (not that that ever happens). They are brightly colored and patterned to warn potential attackers that they are dangerous. The poison is stored in glands on their skin, so any animal that ignores the warning signals and tries to take a bite will get a nasty shock. Even if the frog is badly injured or killed, its attacker, if it survives, is unlikely to attack a similar-looking frog again. This might mean that the original frog's relatives—perhaps even its own children—stand a good chance of being spared in the future.

A tiny poison dart frog can contain enough poison to kill ten people.

THE BEAUTIFUL BUT DEADLY AWARD

THE BEAUTIFUL BUT DEADLY AWARD GOES TO THE POISON DART FROG

Poison dart frogs harvest poison from the animals they eat, such as ants, termites, and mites.

Not all poison dart frogs are deadly. Some just taste bad, which is enough to put off hungry animals.

Some hunters in South America smear the tips of their hunting darts with frog poison, which is how the frogs got their name.

A poison dart frog's defenses don't always work: at least one kind of snake is immune to the poison and specializes in feeding on the frogs.

There are around 170 different kinds of poison dart frog. They mostly live on the ground in damp forests. Many of them are very rare.

1.

Strawberry poison dart frogs go to huge efforts to look after their young. The female lays eggs on a leaf, and the male waters them for ten days with water from his bottom!

2.

The eggs hatch into tadpoles, which the female carries on her back one at a time to somewhere with water.

3.

She then feeds them for a month with special eggs filled with poison, which the tadpoles absorb. This means they are already protected when they turn into froglets.

The NOISY AWARDS

Most animals make a noise. Some animals, such as bats and toothed whales, use sound to find their way around, but most use it to communicate with other animals, especially members of their own species.

SUPERB LYREBIRD *Menura novaehollandiae*
Best song award

Category: birds | **Found in**: Australia | **Lives for:** up to 20 years | **Eats:** insects and other small animals

Birds are talented singer-songwriters, and the superb lyrebird has a good claim to being the champion of champions. It can produce an extraordinary array of sounds. As well as having its own distinctive songs, it is an expert copycat and can mimic virtually every other sound; other birds, chain saws, crying babies, and fire alarms. Both male and female lyrebirds sing, but males spend longer doing so, especially at the start of the breeding season, when they are defending their territories and trying to attract mates. At this time, they may sing for four hours every day.

PISTOL SHRIMP *Alpheidae*
The knock-out award

Category: crustaceans | **Found in**: seawaters worldwide; a few in freshwater | **Lives for:** one year | **Eats:** small animals

Like coquí frogs, underwater pistol shrimps are just an inch long, but they can make a truly impressive—and deadly—sound; one of the loudest in the ocean. One of their two claws is much bigger than the other and can be snapped shut at high speed. As it closes, it sends out a jet of water that creates a bubble of air behind it. The bubble almost immediately implodes with a bang, sending out a sound wave that can stun or kill small animals nearby.

WOODPECKER *Picidae*
Drumming award

Category: birds | **Found in:** all continents, except Antarctica | **Lives for:** up to 20 years | **Eats:** mostly insects, sometimes nuts and fruit, and tree sap

Woodpeckers don't exactly have a song. Instead, they make funny trills, cackles, whistles, and weird laughs. They also love to drum. They tap out rhythms with their beaks, usually on tree trunks and branches, but also on house chimneys, metal posts, and rain gutters. They can drum incredibly quickly—thirty beats or more a second—and very loudly, especially when drumming on something hollow, which they do whenever possible. You would think that they would get headaches from this, but their thick skull bones are filled with tiny air holes that act as shock-absorbers.

PUERTO RICAN COQUÍ *Eleutherodactylus coqui*
Deafening chorus award

Category: amphibians | **Found in:** Puerto Rico, USA | **Lives for:** up to six years | **Eats:** insects

The loudest frog on record is the Puerto Rican coquí. Only the males sing, and they do it at night from perches above ground level. They call to attract females and warn off males. Their song has two parts, the "co" and the "quí," and experiments have shown that other males react to the first part and females to the second. When two males approach each other, they start a calling duel. The one with the strongest "co" wins, and the other male leaves.

55

CHEETAH

Category: mammals | **Found in:** Africa and Iran | **Lives for:** 14 years in the wild |
Eats: carnivore

There is no argument as to what the fastest animal on land is: it's the cheetah.

They can run at almost 65 mph. They use their speed when hunting, and their favorite food is the pronghorn, which look similar to an antelope. These cats are not built for endurance, however, and only ever run this quickly for short bursts. Like other wild cats, they generally ambush their prey, carefully stalking it and sometimes getting as close as 50 feet away, before springing into action. Antelopes remain constantly on the alert for this kind of danger, and the intended victim will quickly set off, literally running for its life, twisting and turning to try to dodge its pursuer. If the cheetah has not overtaken it within 1,500 feet or so, it is likely to escape, as cheetahs rarely pursue their prey farther than this. The unlucky ones are brought down and quickly suffocated before being eaten at leisure.

Cheetahs rarely run at their maximum possible speed when pursuing prey, normally reaching around 35 mph or so. Instead, they rely on their incredible maneuverability, in particular their ability to slow down quickly and make sharp turns without losing their balance. This makes them just as good at hunting in scrubby and wooded areas, where they have to dodge trees and plants, as they are when sprinting in open savannas.

The cheetah accelerates three times faster than an Olympic sprinter, going from 0 to 60 mph in three seconds.

The
SUPER
SPRINTER
AWARD

THE SPRINTER AWARD GOES TO THE CHEETAH

After lions, cheetahs are the most sociable cats. They hunt together and share their kills.

Cheetahs have ridged pads on their feet that help them to grip when they turn—just like spiked running shoes.

A cheetah can cover 22 feet in one stride.

Cheetahs only hunt every couple of days. The rest of the time they rest or stroll around at 2 mph.

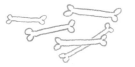

ZZZZZz

Cheetahs are always keeping an eye out for possible prey and for animals that might attack their cubs, such as lions, hyenas, and leopards.

Other fast land animals include springbok and Thomson's gazelles, both among the cheetah's favorite foods. Cheetahs are faster over short distances, and they can't keep up their speed for long.

North American pronghorns are very fast. There are no fast predators left in North America, but pronghorns evolved their running ability to escape a now-extinct cat that resembled cheetahs.

DUNG BEETLE

Category: insects | Found in: most places, except Antarctica | Lives for: up to three years | Eats: dung

Dung beetles are very strong and spend their lives pushing poop around.

They do a hugely important job in stopping poop piling up everywhere. For them poop isn't a waste product—it's a lifeline. They lay their eggs in it, and the young hatch out and feed on it as larvae. The adults don't eat it themselves—they usually don't eat anything. Instead, they nourish themselves on the liquid that oozes out of it.

Most dung beetles roll poop into balls and push it into a hole in the ground. The female then lays her eggs on top of it. Sometimes the pair puts one or two more balls on top, before covering everything with soil.

Rolling dung balls can be hard work, so it's no surprise that dung beetles are very strong for their size. Some male dung beetles can push a dung ball 50 times its own weight up a steep slope, while their mate hitches a ride on top. The strongest dung beetle on record can push loads that are over 1,000 times its body weight. They also use their strength to fend off male competitors. Males will enter the tunnels that the females have dug, but if another male is already in there, they will try to remove each other. The strongest one wins!

A dung beetle can push a ball of dung up to 1,000 times its weight.

THE SMALL BUT STRONG AWARD GOES TO THE DUNG BEETLE

Some dung beetles hang about near piles of dung waiting for a chance to steal balls from other beetles.

As water evaporates, the air on top of the ball becomes cool. The beetles climb up onto the balls to cool down.

The ancient Egyptians regarded dung beetles—also known as scarabs—as sacred. They carved scarab-shaped jewels out of precious stones.

A dung beetle pushes its dung ball backward using its back legs. Its front legs are armed with serrations to give it a strong grip on the ground as it pushes.

At night dung beetles can navigate using the Milky Way (the band of starry light seen in the night sky) to guide themselves. They are the first animals known to do this.

If a dung beetle becomes confused and loses its sense of direction, it will climb on the ball and do a twirling dance to reorientate itself.

There are more than 5,000 different kinds of dung beetle, ranging in size from just 5 mm to over 2 inches. As far as we know, all of them are pretty strong!

VULTURE

Category: birds | Found in: the Americas, Southern Europe, Asia, and Africa |
Lives for: at least 45 years in the wild | Eats: mainly carrion (rotting meat)

On the whole, vultures don't get a very good press. Many people regard them as ugly, and the fact that they're often seen around dead animals can make them seem sinister. In reality, they do an incredibly useful job.

Most kinds feed on the remains of animals that have been killed by predators, or that have died from natural causes. By clearing these remains away, vultures play an important part in controlling the spread of disease.

In India, millions of cows roam the countryside. These cows are considered sacred and usually die of natural causes. Until recently, vast numbers of slender-billed, white-rumped, and Indian vultures fed on the dead cows. However, in the 1990s, vulture populations in India began to decline, which led to carcasses remaining in fields, rotting away and often contaminating drinking water. These carcasses spread diseases like anthrax and the plague. Scavengers such as feral dogs and rats started to increase, but they are much less efficient at clearing away carcasses. Everything fell apart without vultures!

A vulture may be known as a scavenger, but it is actually doing us all a favor.

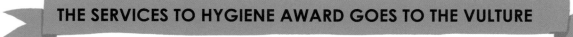

THE SERVICES TO HYGIENE AWARD GOES TO THE VULTURE

A vulture can gobble down 2 pounds of meat in a minute. It takes half an hour for a flock of them to strip a cow carcass.

Vultures have very acid liquid in their stomach, which kills bacteria and breaks down meat fast, before it can start to rot. This makes them unlikely to get sick from their food.

Vultures can roam over enormous distances—sometimes thousands of square miles—looking for food.

The palm-nut vulture is unusual because it is mostly vegetarian. It eats the nuts of oil and raffia palms, although occasionally it will have a crab or frog as a snack.

Many vultures are virtually bald, with just a thin covering of short feathers on their head and neck. This helps keep them clean and their bodies at the right temperature.

The bearded vulture specializes in eating crunchy bones and tortoises. It cracks them open by flying to a height and dropping them on rocks.

TORTOISE

Category: reptiles | **Found in:** North and South America, Europe, Asia, Africa, Madagascar, Aldabra, Galapagos Islands | **Lives for:** ages! (200 years or more) | **Eats:** mainly plants

Quite a lot of animals can live to a good age. Among land animals, the oldest that we know about belong to one family of reptiles—the tortoise.

At least three different tortoises are known to have lived for at least 150 years. Possibly the oldest was a male called Adwaita, who lived in Alipore Zoo in Kolkata, India, from 1875 until 2006.

Harriet was a Galapagos giant tortoise, who lived in Brisbane Botanic Gardens, Australia, from 1860 until she died in 2006. She is thought to have been collected by the scientist Charles Darwin when he visited the Galapagos Islands in 1835, making her well over 170.

Tu'i Malila was a radiated tortoise from Madagascar, who lived in the gardens of the royal palace in Tonga in the South Pacific from at least the early 19th century until 1965. She was said to have been given as a present to the royal family of Tonga by the explorer James Cook when he visited the kingdom in 1777.

The CENTENARIAN AWARD

Tortoises age well. A 120-year-old tortoise can be as healthy as a 20-year-old tortoise.

THE CENTENARIAN AWARD GOES TO THE TORTOISE

The smallest tortoise is only about 4 inches long and the biggest can reach nearly 6 feet. All of them can live for a long time.

Tortoises go on growing throughout their lives, although the older they get, the slower they grow.

Unlike mammals, tortoises don't seem to become susceptible to illness as they age.

Like other reptiles, tortoises can go for months at a time without eating.

Tortoises are the longest-lived land animals, but some marine animals can outlast them.

Greenland sharks: 400 years old.

A black coral: 4000 years old.

An ocean quahog clam: 507 years old.

63

OSTRICH

Category: birds | **Native to:** Africa | **Lives for:** around 40 years | **Diet:** omnivore

Ostriches are the largest birds alive—a big male can stand nearly 10 feet tall and weigh 350 pounds. So perhaps it's not surprising that they lay the world's biggest eggs.

Their eggs are up to 6 inches long and weigh 3 pounds, and are the equivalent of 24 chicken eggs. But there's a twist; an ostrich egg may be the biggest egg around, but it is the smallest egg in relation to the size of the bird.

As you might expect, ostrich nests are pretty big, too. Often several females lay their eggs in the same nest. Ostrich eggs, like other bird's eggs, need to be incubated—that is, kept at an even temperature, neither too hot nor too cold. An ostrich can only incubate around 20 eggs at a time. The female who does the daytime incubation can recognize her own eggs, and if there are too many eggs in the nest, she rolls the ones laid by other females to the sides, where they have much less chance of hatching.

The
AMAZING
EGG
AWARD

OSTRICH EGG

An ostrich egg is the size of 24 chicken eggs!

THE AMAZING EGG AWARD GOES TO THE OSTRICH

Cavemen used to use the white surface of the eggs as canvases to paint and engrave pictures onto.

They are so unusually large that sometimes they are displayed as natural sculptures.

They can hold up to one liter of liquid, so hunter-gatherers used to use them as water flasks.

The unusual thickness of the shell means that they can be made into beads for jewelry.

Ostrich   Emu   Cassowary   Penguin   Dalmatian pelican

Ostriches are the largest birds alive, but here are some other close contenders, along with their eggs.

Ostrich shells are thick so that they don't break under the weight of their parents when they are incubating the eggs.

Elephant birds would have also laid very big eggs, but they became extinct around 1,000 years ago. Their eggs would have been a tempting food for early settlers, and this could be one of the main reasons for the birds' disappearance.

The DISGUISE AWARDS

Unlike plants, which can make their own food through photosynthesis, all animals have to eat. Predators—animals that eat other animals—have evolved all sorts of ways of catching their food, while prey animals (which includes many predators themselves) have developed a host of ways of trying to avoid being eaten. Disguise and deception play a big part in all this. Here are some of the most amazing ways animals have come up with to fool other animals.

CARIBBEAN REEF SQUID *Sepioteuthis sepioidea*
The now-you-see-me-now-you-don't award

Category: mollusks | **Found in:** Western Atlantic, Caribbean Sea, and Gulf of Mexico | **Lives for:** six months | **Eats:** small fishes and shrimps

For animals that swim about in the open water, life is risky because they have nowhere to hide from predators. To get around this problem, the Caribbean reef squid has created some unique survival tricks. When threatened by a predatory fish, it squirts out a cloud of black ink to hide behind. The ink is mixed with a sticky substance that holds it together in a squid-shaped mass. It also contains chemicals that smell like food, so the fish is likely to attack the inky cloud while the squid quickly makes its escape.

PEACOCK FLOUNDER *Bothus lunatus*
The quick-change artist award

Category: fish | **Found in:** tropical Atlantic Ocean | **Lives for:** up to ten years | **Eats:** Fishes, crabs, and other crustaceans

A lot of animals try to blend into their surroundings and have markings that match their environment. Some of these, mostly underwater animals, can change color depending on where they are. Flounder are very good at this—some of them can even imitate checkerboard patterns in aquariums. They are often speedy, too: the peacock flounder can change its appearance completely in a couple of seconds.

SCARLET KINGSNAKE *Lampropeltis elapsoides*
The con-artist award

Category: reptiles | **Found in:** southeast and east USA | **Lives for:** 10–15 years | **Eats:** mostly small lizards, also small rodents and eggs

To warn predators, some animals use bright markings that say "Keep away, I'm poisonous" or "I will give you a nasty bite." Highly venomous American coral snakes do this with red, yellow, and black rings around their bodies. The non-poisonous scarlet kingsnake, which lives in the same places as coral snakes, has very similar markings that fools its predators into thinking it's dangerous.

ORCHID MANTIS *Hymenopus coronatus*
The plant-impersonator award

Category: insects | **Found in:** Southeast Asia | **Lives for:** around eight months | **Eats:** other insects

The southeast Asian orchid mantis is a predatory insect that looks just like an exotic pink flower. It stands near flowers of the same color and tries to blend in. Insects such as bees and hoverflies that feed on flower pollen and nectar come by looking for a meal and find they become one instead. The mantis has another trick for attracting snacks: it produces a signal much like the one that Asian honeybees use to tell each other they have found something tasty. When bees come to look for food, the mantis gobbles them up. Cunning!

LION'S MANE JELLYFISH

Category: cnidarians | Found in: the Arctic, north Atlantic and north Pacific Oceans | Lives for: probably around one year | Eats: other animals

Jellyfish don't have arms or legs, or tails for that matter, but the lion's mane jellyfish does have tentacles aplenty.

These odd animals have a bell-shaped body with a single opening on the underside fringed with tentacles. The lion's mane has incredibly tong tentacles. The longest ever recorded were 120 feet (that's longer than the biggest blue whale). Each one of these jellyfish have up to 1,200 tentacles.

Like other jellyfish, lion's mane jellyfish don't use their tentacles for swimming. They do that with elegant pulsations of their bell. They also cover long distances simply by drifting in ocean currents. Instead, the tentacles are used for catching food. They are covered in huge numbers of stinging cells called cnidocytes, which are set off when they come into contact with solid objects. When other sea animals become tangled in the tentacles, the cnidocytes inject poison into them, which kills or paralyzes them. The victims are then drawn up through the opening in the center of the tentacles, into a gut-like space in the jellyfish's bell, where they are digested. Any undigested remains are then expelled out through the same opening.

The lion's mane jellyfish has tentacles longer than a blue whale.

THE TANGLIEST TENTACLES AWARD GOES TO THE LION'S MANE JELLYFISH

One of the lion's mane jellyfish's main foods is other jellyfish.

Lion's mane jellyfish are themselves an important food for the endangered leatherback turtle.

A lion's mane jellyfish has no brain and no proper eyes, but it does have a nervous system and cells that can sense light and dark.

Lion's mane jellyfish are mostly found in cold waters in the far north, but in late summer and autumn they often drift farther south.

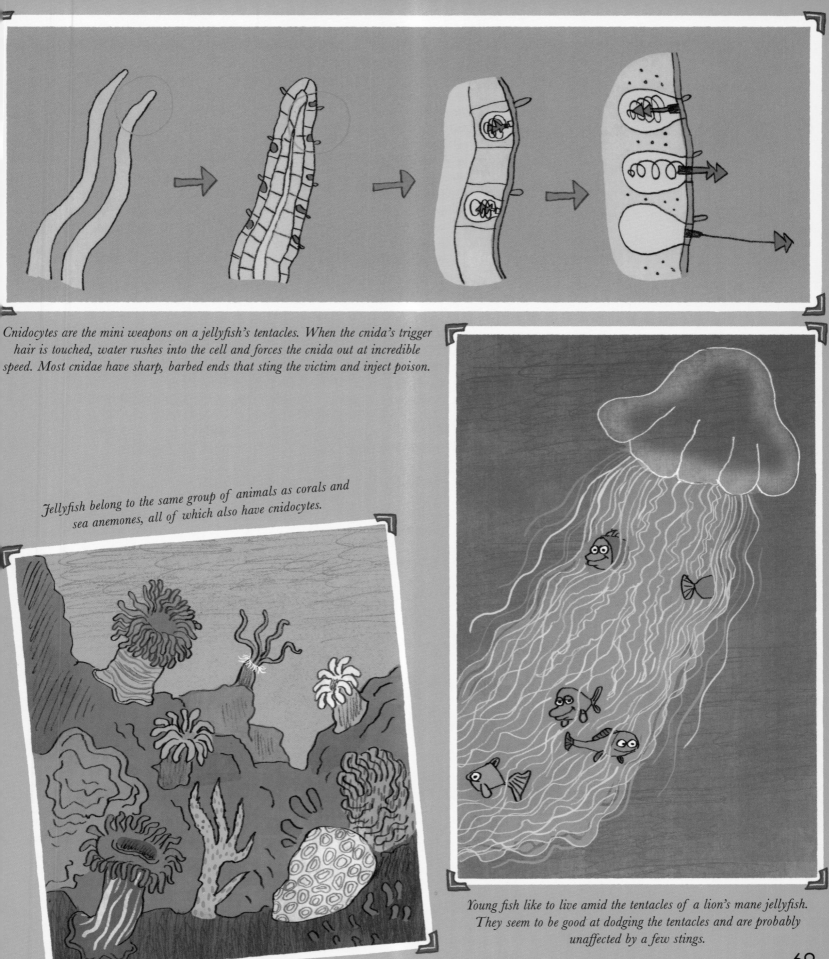

Cnidocytes are the mini weapons on a jellyfish's tentacles. When the cnida's trigger hair is touched, water rushes into the cell and forces the cnida out at incredible speed. Most cnidae have sharp, barbed ends that sting the victim and inject poison.

Jellyfish belong to the same group of animals as corals and sea anemones, all of which also have cnidocytes.

Young fish like to live amid the tentacles of a lion's mane jellyfish. They seem to be good at dodging the tentacles and are probably unaffected by a few stings.

AXOLOTL

Category: amphibians | **Found in:** Mexico | **Lives for:** at least 17 years | **Eats:** small underwater animals, mainly worms and fishes

All animals change and grow after they are born but very few can regrow entire parts of their body.

Many animals, including humans, stop growing when they are adults, although parts such as hair and nails continue to grow. In all animals, at least some of the cells that make up the body's tissues and organs are gradually replaced throughout life. Most adult animals, however, can't replace major parts of themselves, such as legs or arms, if these are lost or damaged in accidents. Newts and salamanders are different. Some have the extraordinary ability to regenerate, and none more so than the axolotl, which is a kind of salamander found in lakes near Mexico City.

Like frogs, axolotls are amphibians, and like frogs, when they are young they live entirely underwater and breathe through gills. As they grow, they lose their gills, replacing them with air-breathing lungs. Axolotls are unusual in that they keep their gills and stay underwater their whole lives. As adults, they look like giant salamander larvae, although they are perfectly capable of breeding. They may be good at regeneration because in some ways they never quite grow up.

Even though these animals can regrow whole limbs, they are still virtually extinct because of human pollution.

THE MAGICAL HEALER AWARD GOES TO THE AXOLOTL

Axolotls can grow entire new legs, jaws, tails, and even parts of their eyes, brain, and heart.

It takes an axolotl between one and three months to grow a new, fully working leg.

Axolotls are common in captivity, but are now very rare in the wild.

The first live axolotls outside Mexico arrived in Paris in 1864. Most of the captive axolotls around today are descended from these.

GIANT CLAM

Category: mollusks | Found in: coral reefs in warm shallow waters in the Indian and Pacific Ocean regions | Lives for: over 100 years | Eats: tiny sea organisms and food produced by algae

Our skeleton is very useful, but if you want to be protected from incoming danger, a skeleton on the outside is better.

This is called an exoskeleton, and that is what the giant clam has. Its hard shell serves both as a support for the animal's soft parts and as protection.

Some animals have exoskeletons that are jointed and flexible, like beetles and other insects, and crustaceans such as crabs and lobsters. Others are completely rigid and immobile. Gastropod mollusks such as snails, conches, cowries, and their relatives have shells of this sort. Bivalve mollusks, such as clams, oysters, and mussels, have something between the two. Their shells consist of two parts joined together with a flexible hinge. The heaviest of these, and the heaviest exoskeleton of any living animal, belongs to the giant clam, which is one of the most spectacular inhabitants of coral reefs in the Indian and Pacific Oceans. The biggest-known giant clam shell, collected in the 19th century, is more than 4 feet across and weighs an amazing 500 pounds.

The Heaviest SHELL AWARD

The giant clam is a rock-hard heavyweight champion.

THE HEAVIEST SHELL AWARD GOES TO THE GIANT CLAM

A giant clam has more than 3,000 eyes, though each one is very simple and can't see in detail.

Like oysters and mollusks, giant clams can produce pearls, although they have a dull surface not at all like the ones used in jewelry.

Giant clam meat is very popular (and expensive) in Asia and the Pacific region.

72

Adult giant clams are fixed in position. When threatened, they use powerful muscles called adductors to close their shells, squirting jets of water out as they do so.

Giant clams produce most of their food. They grow tiny creatures that survive on sunlight.

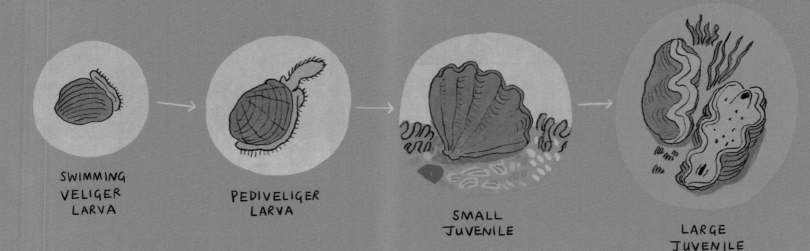

SWIMMING VELIGER LARVA

PEDIVELIGER LARVA

SMALL JUVENILE

LARGE JUVENILE

Giant clams start life as eggs. When they hatch, the larvae swim around and don't look anything like their parents. After several days, they settle on the reef floor, where they turn into miniature clams. The young clams can still move around, using a foot that they also use for scooping up food. When they have found a suitable spot, they settle down there for the rest of their lives.

POLAR BEAR

Category: marine mammals | **Native to:** the Arctic | **Lives for:** max. 45 years | **Diet:** carnivore

Polar bears really love the ice. No other animal is so well suited to life on the huge expanses of it that covers the Arctic Ocean for much of the year.

Their favorite food is ringed and bearded seals, both of which are common in the Arctic Ocean. The seals spend a lot of time underwater. When they are hunting under the ice, they occasionally pop up to the surface to breathe when they find a hole. This is where a polar bear waits, crouching patiently until a seal pops out. As the seal nears the surface, it breathes out, ready to take another breath. The polar bear smells its breath and quickly plunges a front paw into the water, flipping the seal onto the ice. The bears also stalk seals that are resting on the ice.

Polar bears love to hunt, but with the ice disappearing earlier and earlier every year, they are forced to find other sources of food. Some move inland, scavenging on rubbish dumps, and raiding the nests of geese and other birds. Some end up going without food for weeks or months, until the sea starts to freeze up again. Polar bears love the ice, and they rely on it, but it's shrinking due to climate change.

A polar bear is a cool customer that loves life on the ice. It is also the biggest carnivore that lives on land.

THE NORTH POLE AWARD GOES TO THE POLAR BEAR

Their thick white coats make excellent camouflage against the white ice and helps insulate them.

They have non-slip soles on their feet to stop them from sliding around on the ice.

They have amazing stamina, which helps when walking long distances in search of food.

They are good at fishing in the holes they make in the ice.

Although a polar bear's fur looks white, it is actually transparent and its skin underneath is black.

Polar bears wait at holes in the ice to try to catch seals when they pop up for a breath of fresh air.

Polar bears are good at diving for fish! They can't spend too long underwater or they get cold.

Once the sea ice melts, a polar bear has to walk inland to scavenge for other sources of food.

INDEX